Dragons Along the Silk Road...and Beyond

Are dragons all alike, no matter where you are in the world?

Dragons Here and There

Mind you, dragons in the West and dragons in the East don't seem to be alike at all at first glance, but…

Dragons Everywhere

You'll find that some dragons far away from you have a strange similarity. Why is that?

**Take a journey
around the world with us and explore dragons
wherever you go**

Workshops by Eilis Flynn and Jacquie Rogers

The Silk Road Myths and Legends Workshop Series
Angels
Demons
Dragons
Faeries
Ghosts
Vampires
Water Beasties
Werewolves and Other Shapeshifters
Bigfeet

The Five Stages of Editing Grief
Geeks and Gamers' Guide to Worldbuilding

Books by Eilis Flynn and Jacquie Rogers

Ghosts Along the Silk Road and Beyond
Dragons Along the Silk Road and Beyond

DRAGONS ALONG THE SILK ROAD AND BEYOND

Based on the series of workshops presented by
Eilis Flynn and Jacquie Rogers

Eilis Flynn
and
Jacquie Rogers

Dragons Along the Silk Road and Beyond

For Mike and Mark.
Thank you.

Chapters

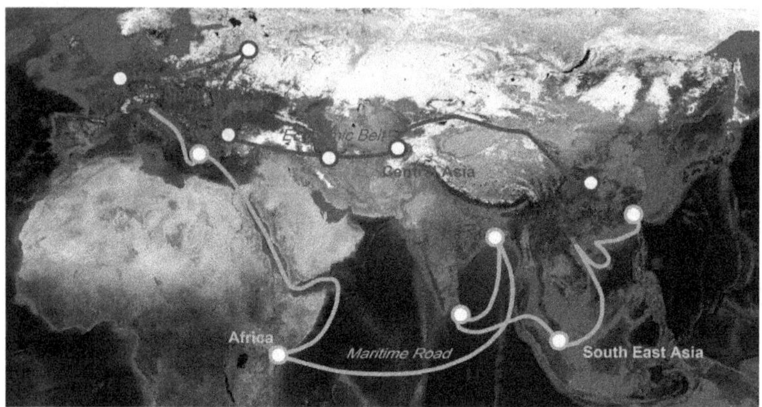

A map for the Silk Road journey.

Introduction
Here, There Be Dragons

No matter where you go in the world, take a look at the folktales and the myths in the culture you're in, and more likely than not you'll find the mention of a dragon or two. Some of them will be described as green or gold or red, some of them will be described as having wings and some won't, some of them will be described as having five claws, some four, some only three, some even with more than one head. The details don't matter, though, because it's clear that you've encountered yet another story about dragons.

Like ghosts, stories about dragons can be found all over the world. Ranging from the dragons that play an important part in Chinese culture all the way to the legend of Quetzalcoatl found in Mesoamerican culture, they are all around us, whether or not we recognize them by name. Stories about dragons have been around as long as human society itself, and like all myths and legends, they reflect the society in which they can be found.

The term "dragon" itself is of Greek origin, meaning "a serpent or python," and it can also mean "to see clearly." Wherever the legend of the dragon appears, they represent some part of society, culture, and wisdom (thus the "seeing clearly" reference), since dragons are also often referred to as having spiritual qualities. Some part a god and all parts myth, dragons seem to expand and contract to whatever the region and culture in which they appear seem to need. There's the dragon of the Western lore, hoarding treasure and fighting to keep it, but there's also the dragon of the Eastern part of the world, in which knowledge is all-important. Sometimes the goals of the dragons are reversed, curiously. Sometimes they talk, sometimes they don't.

What we found interesting (okay, we found all of it interesting) is how the dragon myths were both threatening and soothing. The earliest stories had the dragons evil in Sumerian myth, born of demons and sludge and fighting the earliest warriors. But soon thereafter the dragons become somewhat less evil, protective of the environment, even, before the stories made them heroes. They become what they need to be, at any place and time.

Join us as we take another trip around the world, this time in search of dragons. Whether you make use of the legend of the dragon when you're writing your own stories doesn't matter, because you'll find that examining the legend of the dragon up close is really an examination of yourself and your story.

Stories about dragons appear in one form or another all around the world. The physical description of the dragon varies as well as its abilities, but two things don't change: that it is serpentine or reptilian in form and it has magical abilities or possessions that make it a target for knights or warriors. The most familiar dragons are from Europe and Asia, but Quetzalcoatl of Central America is clearly from the dragon family, and the drawings and descriptions you'll run across indicate that yes, that's a dragon.

No matter where you go in the world, take a good look at the folktales and the myths, and more likely than not you'll find a mention of a creature that sounds a lot like one you've probably heard about all your life, but a bit different. That could be a faery, an angel, a demon, or even vampires or werewolves or ghosts. In the case of dragons, you could even have heard a story about a sea-based creature that somehow seems unbelievable, yet—not. It could describe a giant creature and it could even describe the thing with wings or fins, but you could swear you've heard the same story but with a different description. They can't all possibly be true. Right?

Funny thing is, those stories can sound mighty similar to each other, even though they may originate in cultures and places thousands of miles apart. For example, there are stories about dragons in Western Europe, in Asia, and in Native American culture. They all have wildly varying descriptions, but judging by the stories, they're all clearly supposed to be dragons. You may dismiss the coincidence, since dragons aren't real (as far as we know), but here's the thing: There are stories and descriptions of such mythological creatures of all stripes and colors all around the world. How's that possible?

This is something that any anthropology major takes for granted, of course. But it's not necessarily something that anybody really thinks about. But that's only because nobody's pointed it out. That's why we're here!

This book was born from a series of workshops when we realized there were variations of the same myths all around the world. Eilis was an anthropology major, so she was familiar with the concept that cultures in the same region or came from the same roots would usually have similar legends and myths, and she'd already spent some time studying them, noting how they changed as the cultures did. She was also familiar with Japanese culture, having spent her childhood there. Jacquie had done research on European mythologies for her series of fantasy romances. When we realized that the people around us were always talking about the variations of fantastical creatures, we decided to combine all that "book learnin'," as Jacquie would say, and look at the myths along the Silk Road and beyond.

And before we get started, let us tell you about the Silk Road. Traditionally, the Silk Road was a series of important trading routes going over land and sea that existed long before the Christian era began. A *lot* of trade occurred along those routes, bringing silks and spices and more from the East to the West, and vice versa.

The Silk Road connected a region of China with Asia Minor and the Mediterranean, a route that was more than 5,000 miles long—a fair distance these days, but unimaginable back then, fraught with danger and a journey that took a very, very long time for a round trip. The Silk Road had northern routes and southern routes, and the goods were transported from places as far away as the Philippines and Thailand and Brunei, all the way to Italy and Portugal and even Scandinavia.

Not only were silks and spices moved along these routes, so was culture, language, and even technology, and that meant Asian concepts and items were introduced to Europe, and vice versa. We'll see how those ideas began and changed as we travel from region to region, changing bit by bit until those concepts end up drastically different when compared side by side.

In the research that we conducted about dragons along the Silk Road and around the world, a few details stood out that separated the dragons of the Western world from the dragons of the East. Jacquie will start us out by telling us about those Western dragons and then Eilis will look at the Eastern ones.

Intrigued? Let us take you on a walk around the world to examine those myths, and see how they shift, change, and evolve as we travel.

Ready? Let's go!

Eilis Flynn
Jacquie Rogers

Image of Quetzalcoatl, the feathered serpent-god of Mesoamerican myth.

Chapter 1
Dragons from Hollywood Across the Americas

"The dragons of the mountains have scales of a golden color, and in length excel those of the plain, and they have bushy beards, which also are of a golden hue; and their eye is sunk deep under the eyebrow, and emits a terrible and ruthless glance."
—Greek scholar Philostratus (c. AD 170-245)

Folklore has generally placed dragons in the same categories as the bad guys—fierce, powerful, greedy, vengeful, and with a keen appetite for virgin maidens, especially princesses. But they're also empowered with intelligence, sometimes considered the keepers of knowledge, and are often key players in creation stories, such as Tiamat of the Babylonians. (Fun fact: Tiamat is one of the few references we've found that expressly notes the dragon as female.) We'll get into that later.

Hollywood likes to play around with folklore. In the *Shrek* movies, ogres are the good guy and lady, and the faery godmother is selfish and evil. The dragons in the 2010 movie *How to Train Your Dragon* are misunderstood creatures. The Vikings feared the dragons, who stole their sheep. What the humans didn't know was that those dragons were being blackmailed by a big, bad, dragon, and if they didn't bring him sheep, he would eat them. So these dragons were basically good, and once the problem was resolved, Vikings and dragons lived Happily Ever After.

We can't have a discussion about dragons in Hollywood without mentioning *Dragonheart*, a 1996 release. Here's IMDB's description:

The last dragon and a disillusioned dragon-slaying knight must cooperate to stop an evil king who was given partial immortality.

You just have to root for the dragon when he has Sean Connery's golden voice. This isn't the best movie ever made, but is a guilty pleasure for some of us.

(And of course there's a fearsome dragon in *Beowulf*, but we'll talk about that in the next chapter.)

And then there's the post-apocalyptic *Reign of Fire* (2002), with Matthew McConaughey and Christian Bale. From IMDB:

A brood of fire-breathing dragons emerges from beneath the earth and begins setting everything ablaze, establishing dominance over the planet.

Some caveats: A good share of the dragon "lore" you find on the Internet is actually gamer lore and sometimes it's difficult to separate the gamers' sites from actual folklore. Gamers are notorious for doing solid research, then adding their own spin to fit their story world, and sometimes it's seamless.

Not only that, there's a significant body of work on the web, some of which is used here, from people who don't believe dinosaurs were created before humans and that they walked the Earth together. Most of these are called "Forbidden History" or something like that. This book has nothing to do with religion—we simply pulled bits and pieces of pertinent information wherever we found it, and it's up to you to determine validity for the purposes of your own curiosity.

Dragons vary as widely as cultures do. Although many Western dragons are brutal, ignorant creatures who kill and eat humans, others are ancient, wise creatures more akin to those found in the Far East, which we will discuss later. For now, let's explore the mighty dragons of North America before we head to Europe.

Mishipizheu
The sea monster Mishipizheu is a dragon-like creature of the Ojibwe who lived on the shores of Lake Superior. Other peoples around the Great Lakes and Mississippi Valley incorporated Mishipizheu into their lore as well. This creature is also called the Underwater Panther—it has the scales of a snake, the body of a feline (panther or lynx), the horns of a bison, and spikes on its back. It's also known as the Great Horned Lynx.

There's a YouTube video that shows the Ojibwe's pictographs of Mishipizheu. Be patient, because it's nine minutes long and there are only two "scenes" that are of interest for this discussion. The first pictographs are shown at about 3:45, so be ready to hit pause. The next come at about 6:00, and the last few minutes are just scenery (but pretty).
http://www.youtube.com/watch?v=ShyHwMzEI_E&feature=player_embedded

Mishipizheu live in the deepest lakes and rivers, are said to rule the weather, are fearsome, and its breath can bring death. They're in opposition to the stories about

Thunderbird, bringing balance. Which brings up:

Thunderbird
The Lakota call him Wakiya, the Ojibwe call him Animikii. Why is the Thunderbird in a dragon class? Because their lore and supernatural powers are very similar to European dragons in some respects. (See Quetzalcoatl as a comparison.)

This is a huge bird, sometimes horned, who creates thunder from flapping his wings and shoots lightning (or fire) from his eyes. Passamaquaddy lore up in Maine figures the Thunderbird in its creation legend. The Quillayutes (of the Pacific Coast) attribute the Thunderbird to saving the People from Killer Whale and warding off starvation, so the Thunderbird can be found all over the place.

From *The Short Encyclopedia of Hotcâk (Winnebago) Myth, Legend, and Folklore*, by Richard L. Dieterle:
Thunderbirds are powerful and warlike avian spirits who animate the gray clouds with thunder and lightning. Together with the Waterspirits, they were the first spirits that Earthmaker created. Their name, Wak'âdja, means "Divine Ones." On the model of other tribes, they are conventionally called "Thunderbirds," since they alone possess lightning. Their basic somatic form runs the gamut of several species of birds, the hawk and the eagle being the most common. However, they are far stronger in build and have polychrome plumage that gives them a magnificent appearance unrivaled by the birds of earth. Their voices are like the sounds of flutes, recalling both the whistle of wind and the voices of raptors.

If you put a reptilian body on this creature, voila! you'd have a European dragon.

A little farther up the continent we run into Manipogo or ogopogo, up in Lake Manitoba. From all accounts it's a great big snake (specifically, serpentine cryptid), with a lot in common with the Loch Ness monster over in Europe.

Piasa

Just as fearsome is the Piasa, of which a pictograph was described in 1673 by Father Jacques Marquette:

They are as large as a calf; they have horns on their heads like those of a deer, a horrible look, red eyes, a beard like a tiger's, a face somewhat like a man's, a body covered with scales, and so long a tail that it winds all around the body, passing above the head and going back between the legs, ending in a fish's tail.

Doesn't sound very bird-like to me, but that's the thing about dragons. This creature's legend has been lost in time, and the myth that is generally cited was probably made up in the mid-1800s by author John Russell, and is undocumented.

Quetzalcoatl

There are other serpentine creatures noted in the Americas but in Mexico thereabouts, the feathered serpent Quetzalcoatl ruled supreme. Translated literally, Quetzalcoatl means "plumed serpent." He is all-powerful and takes many forms, including the sun, wind, morning star, and the high priest Topiltzin. Quetzalcoatl created humanity by sprinkling his blood on the remains of the previous human race. From this came the current people. As a result, Quetzalcoatl is regarded as the creator of the modern age.

From the descriptions—particularly the "feathered" part—Quetzalcoatl sounds as if it might have even been the last of the dinosaurs, since there have been some fossil evidence about feathers instead of scales for some kinds! Keep that in mind for your stories—the father of the humans *and* the last of his kind!

Traveling south to South America, we have folklore that both sounds familiar and not. The *coco* (or *cuca* for the feminine; also *cucuy*) has dragonish qualities. The Wikipedia entry refers to the coco as a "ghost-monster," largely found in Hispanic and Portuguese-based cultures; the myth probably began in the Iberian region of Europe (as in Spain and Portugal). The creature is described as a female alligator taken humanoid form. The name is derived from the Portuguese *coca*, meaning—yes, that's right, dragon.

The cuca's appearance isn't necessarily the scary thing—although it's apparently horrible to look at—but what he/she does is, certainly. It is the local bogeyman, known as a child eater and kidnapper. Like so many myths designed to keep children under control, it is constantly on the lookout for childish misbehavior, often keeping tabs by sitting up on the roof. (In a number of societies around the world, there's a reference to a supernatural being, bad or good, keeping tabs from up on the roof.) Wiki refers to the cuca as the opposite of the guardian angel, so it's basically a demonic dragon. There's more about the cuca, coming up in the next chapter.

Hollywood and entertainment connections for the cuca, according to Wikipedia, are pervasive in Latin culture, among which are:
• In Wizards of Waverly Place, cucuys are shown to be wealthy Latin bogeymen.
• Ultimate fighter Tony Ferguson calls himself "El Cucuy."
• There's a short film titled *El Cucuy* that premiered at the 2012 SXSW in Austin, TX.
• The story of the cucuy was used to design a maze for Universal Studios in 2013.
• And in the old TV series *Grimm*, the legend of el cucuy

was adapted as a vigilante battling for the rights of women in peril. (We saw the episode and never knew there might be a dragon connection!)

And there's the legend of the ouroboros, familiar and yet not, showing up in South America. It is a common belief among indigenous cultures of the lowlands that the water at the edge of the world are encircled by a snake, often seen as an anaconda, biting its own tail. The ouroboros is connected with dragon lore elsewhere in the world. More about that later.

It's time to pack up our bags and head for Europe, which has its own rich tradition of dragons.

Consider this: Think of the dragon movies that have come out over the years, and the differences in how dragons are depicted. For North American dragons—what dragons have you found? Central and South America—are there other dragons you've noted?

The coat of arms for Moscow, Russia, depicts St. George and the dragon.

Chapter 2
European Dragons

Generally, European dragons are four-legged and live about 1,200 years, taking about 150 years to reach maturity. This version of the dragon breathes fire, stockpiles gold or precious gems, and is also the keeper of knowledge. Welcome to the prototypical Western dragon, on the descriptions of which are based the many tales of dragon derring-do are based.

The typical Western dragon is a large, scaly creature resembling a dinosaur or a large lizard. It usually has wings and can fly, and often it will breathe fire or noxious gases. An alternative name for Western dragons is *wyrm*, an Old English word now evolved to "worm." This term is more commonly used for serpentine, water-dwelling dragons but can be used for any dragon type. Water-dwelling dragons are to be especially common in Britain (and in the East, but more on that later).

In the rest of Europe, most dragons live in caves or mountains (or mountain caves) or hidden away in the forests. They often guard a stash of gold and/or precious jewels, of which they're particularly fond. Some dragons are said to get their powers from the treasure they protect so fiercely. Western dragons are often used to symbolize greed because they don't miss a chance to collect more treasure and are so protective of their hoards of goodies. Fossils play heavily in dragon lore in European stories.

Legend has it that long ago, the marshes near Klagenfurt, Austria, were haunted by a fearsome *Lindwurm*—a serpentlike dragon. It devoured all the people and livestock who ventured its way. Finally, a local ruler called on his knights to destroy the dragon, and after many attempts it was slain. To commemorate the event, a "dragon" skull was placed in the town hall. In 1582, an artist borrowed the skull—really, what looks like actually the fossil remains of an Ice Age woolly rhinoceros—to use as a model in shaping a massive sculpture of the Lindwurm, which still stands in the city today.

The first European representation of what many interpret as a dragon is a bit controversial. The photo was taken by Jack Cuozzo in the Bernifal Cave in France. He claimed that a cave drawing portrayed a dinosaur fighting a mammoth.

Cuozzo claims that whether dinosaur or dragon, apparently someone saw a reptile of some kind fighting with a mammoth, and then this person painted the picture. Neither a dinosaur nor a dragon are immediately identifiable in the image but some claim they can, so we'll leave it to them.

It seems reasonable to believe that the fossils discovered by prehistoric peoples would wend their way into the lore. How can you not be curious about such huge bones? How could you not speculate about such an animal's life and death? Don't we do the same with dinosaurs? There's another writing about a similar situation from Pliny the Elder's *Natural History, Book VII, Chapter XII,* in which dragons described sounded more like a giant constrictor snake…like some of the dragons described in the Far East. More on that later (of course).

Beowulf & the Dragon
The origin of Beowulf is Anglo-Saxon, a story told in an eighth-century poem written in Old English. The poem consists of three stories, and the third story tells of Grendel's combat with a fire dragon. It goes like this: One of Beowulf's servants was in trouble, so he ran away. He stumbled upon a dragon hoard at a burial ground near the town. The gold goblet would be a good bribe to clear his name, so he took it and went back home. When the dragon woke up and found a piece of his treasure gone, he was infuriated. In retaliation, he set fire to the villages in the kingdom.

Here's the IMDB summary of the 2007 movie:
Set against the coming of Christianity, this is the story of the last hero: in 507, a monstrous troll wreaks havoc in the mead hall of the Danish king, Hrothgar. He offers rewards for the death of Grendel, so Beowulf, a great and boastful Geat warrior, arrives with his thanes. Beowulf sets aside his armor and awaits the monster; a fierce battle ensues that leads to Beowulf's entering the watery lair of Grendel's mother, where a devil's bargain awaits. Beowulf returns to Herot, the castle, and becomes king. Jump ahead many years, and the sins of the father are visited upon Beowulf and his kingdom. The hero must face his weakness and be heroic once again. Was the age of demons over?

Of course not. Boy howdy, was there ever a fierce fight to the death! The dragon was a fire dragon, but there are other Norse dragons as well in the tale. Jormungand was the son of Loki, and he was a sea serpent who was so immense, he coiled around entire islands, and in fact is credited with creating the oceans.

Because of his size and being a bit on the obnoxious side, Odin took him to Asgard, where he grew even bigger and more obnoxious. When he grew so large that he encircled Midgard, he bit his own tail (and so he is linked to the Egyptian serpent ouroboros). Jormungand had the distinction of slaying Thor, but at the cost of his own death at Thor's hand.

Another dragon of Norse tales: Nidhogg's favorite meal was the corpses of criminals or those who fostered evil hearts, but if there weren't any dead bad guys around, he'd chow down on the Tree of Life, Yggdrasil. This isn't good since we definitely need the Tree of Life.

There is a third type of dragon in these parts: Fafnir started out human, a young man who coveted his father's treasure. Eventually, he did steal the treasure, which only fueled his greed, turning him into a terrifying dragon, renamed Tere. He amassed even more treasure and guarded it with all his considerable might. Warriors came from far and wide to slay the dragon, since the reward was the dragon's treasure. Sigurd did actually manage to kill Fafnir, but his life in turn was cursed by the treasure.

Heading South
And in England, there's the story of the Knucker Dragon. On England's coast southeast of London is a village called Lyminster, and local lore holds that it had a dragon. The Knucker lived in a bottomless pool that is reputed to have a bounty of treasure at the bottom. (Except if it's bottomless…but who are we to quibble.)

This dragon had a taste for maidens (another common thread in Western dragon lore) and had eaten them all, except for the daughter of the King of Sussex. So you can see, the king was a little worried. We imagine the princess was biting her nails, too.

Anyway, the king put out word that any knight who slew the dragon would be rewarded with the king's daughter in marriage. So a knight did slay the dragon and they all lived happily ever after. Except, of course, for the maidens who had already ben consumed.

There are a few other versions of this story. There's one from the mysteriousbritain website:

…A local lad named Jim Puttock fed the dragon an indigestible pudding, then killed it whilst it was indisposed with a bout of bellyache! He got some of the dragon's blood on his hand and, after wiping his mouth after a celebratory pint of beer, Puttock also died.

And the ancient Celts also used the symbol of the dragon on their battle gear. Even now, the image of a red dragon appears on the flag of Wales.

Iberian Peninsula Dragons
The cuca, as opposed to what we saw in South America, wasn't a bogeyman, or bogeywoman. This female dragon took part in medieval celebrations, and the myth survives to some degree to this day as a part of a regional tournament, battling St. George during the Corpus Christi celebrations in Spain.

During this celebration, the cuca is known as "Santa Coca" and if she defeats St. George, it's going to be a bad year for the crops. If St. George wins by cutting off one of her ears and her tongue, it's going to be a good year for the crops. (Apparently, the local folks cheer for Santa Coca, so make of that what you will.)

According to local legend, the coca/cuca arrived from the sea, and promptly took to devouring young women before being killed by the local young men (again, a familiar thing when it comes to European dragons). The oldest reference to cuca is from 1274, where she appears on the shore. The description could have been for a whale or dolphin or any large fish, distorted through time.

Another description 200 years or so later has a description that suggests a tortoise with a spiked spine, dragon claws, and a head. The story connected to this legend seems to parallel the French story of Tarasque, coming up next.

French Dragons
We have a female dragon named Tarasque, the offspring of the giant serpent Onachus and the water dragon Leviathan. For some reason she chose to live in France. She was said to be larger than a dozen elephants, her scales were impenetrable, her teeth were long as swords and just as sharp, and she breathed fire. You wouldn't want to meet her in a dark alley.

She took what she wanted and ate what she wanted. Humans perceived this as bad since she was eating their food—and them. Warriors and knights from all over the continent tried to slay her, but they were powerless against her massive size, armor, and fire.

This continued for an entire generation, when finally St. Martha came to visit. Using only her faith, purity, and a jug of holy water, she negotiated with Tarasque and brought the now-docile dragon back to town. And the villagers beat the dragon and sliced her up. And that was the end of Tarasque. In honor of the event a church was build in Martha's honor and the town was renamed Tarascon.

Austria—A different take on dragons
Austrian dragons didn't eat virgins and the nobility couldn't be bothered to mess with them, so Austrian dragon lore is a bit different. The story about the dragon and the Venediger goes like this:

Long ago there was a dragon ravaging the small mountain village of Sonntag. One day, a Venediger appeared. He jumped on the dragon and rode off through the valley. From that day on the dragon was never seen again.

What is a *Venediger*, you ask? We were curious too. The word literally means "man from Venice." From about the Middle Ages on, merchants from Venice traveled throughout the Alps to find and buy rock crystals and other minerals, which were cut and sold in Venice. In Alpine folklore, a Venediger is a kind of goblin or dwarf searching for rare crystals and especially gold. Some of them could even turn the water of a secret spring into gold (although in some cases it took five years to fill the magical jar).

This particular myth does not mention any hoard of treasure, nor if the dwarves or goblins were from Venice. But perhaps it was their common love for the treasures of the mountains that established the friendship between the Venediger and the dragon.

Then there's the dragon of Slavic mythology, from all over Eastern Europe. The term *zmey* (from Bulgarian and

Russian), its close relatives *zmiy* (Polish and Ukrainian), and *zmaj* (Serbian, Bosnian, Croatian, Slovene), all have been used to refer to a dragon. It should be noted that all these terms are the masculine form for the word for snake—which traditionally in these languages take the feminine. (There's also a similar creature in Romanian stories, the *zmeu*. In Polish lore, there's another term for dragon, *smok*.) Not only that, there's a Russian tale about a green dragon named Zmey, which has three heads and spits fire.

The dragons of this region are distinct from others in Europe. According to Wikipedia, some Russian dragons symbolize the Mongols. There are some prehistoric structures in Russia near Kiev that are thought to be connected with dragons as symbols of foreigners, so that would make sense. But Russian dragons are determined sorts; many stories involving dragons mention they have heads that grow back if every single head on a multi-headed dragon isn't cut off and the body burned. In Bulgaria, as well as Macedonia, there is another sort of dragon, the *lamya*, which is also described as a hydra-like thing.

Probably the best-known Western dragon didn't even technically live in Europe—he lived in Georgia, on the crossroads of Eastern Europe and Western Asia. Yep, it's… St. George's dragon! We've all heard the legend of St. George's dragon. St. George killing the dragon is also represented on the coat of arms of Moscow.

Most of us have only heard of the slaying version, which I'll recap here, but there's another version as well.

In this version, the village of Cappadocia is ravaged by a hungry dragon. First he eats all their sheep, then demands a maiden. The villagers set up a lottery to determine which virgin has the privilege of being the dragon's next repast. Soon, only the princess remains. She knows her duty and goes willingly to the stake, where she's tied, waiting for the dragon. Good old George shows up (why he didn't care about the other maidens is not part of the story), heroically slays the dragon, and the villagers never had dragon troubles again. The other version starts off the same way, except George didn't slay the dragon, he converted it to Christianity, and they all lived happily ever after.

What can we conclude about Western dragons?

Western dragons come in practically every size, shape, and color, so you're free to choose whatever your fashion sense desires in that regard. In Western lore they're all reptilian, with scales. Some have wings and some don't. Some prefer water and some don't. Let your imagination take you wherever it wants to go.

Consider this: How have you crafted your dragons? What lore have you used, adopted, or just plain made up? Have you used Western dragons or Eastern dragons or both? Do you know the difference? Do any do the tango?

A relief of Tiamat, the Babylonian primordial goddess of the sea.

Chapter 3
Mediterranean and Near Eastern Dragons

The dragons we encounter by the time we get down to the Mediterranean and past the sea have less in common with the dragons we encounter in European culture. In classical Greek culture, one of the earliest mentions of a dragon is from the *Iliad*, where Agamemnon is described as having a blue dragon motif on his sword belt and a three-headed dragon emblem on his breastplate. The color reference is mostly a cultural thing, because that's pretty much the only place we saw anything about blue dragons. And of course, the references to the "sea-monster" or the "leviathan" of the Biblical stories, seem to be close to the idea of the dragon we see elsewhere, once more described as the villain.

Before the Greeks, Romans, or Egyptians, there were the Babylonians and the Sumerians. Sumerian cuneiform is one of the earliest written languages that we know of currently, so it's natural they should have been among the first to record legends of monsters that would later be called dragons. Azag and/or Kur, depending on the source, was/were quite ferocious. The following story was related on about six different websites, so here it is, a bit more succinctly than we encountered it:

A warrior deity, Ninurta was the god of the south wind.

Ninurta sets out to destroy the dragon Kur. They battle time and again, forcing Ninurta to retreat time and again, but eventually, Kur is destroyed. In revenge—for Kur is one of his sons—Absu, the god of fresh water, causes the fields to be flooded with unclean waters. By piling stones over Kur's corpse, Ninurta creates a dam, thus diverting those waters into the Tigris.

Some sources say that Ninurta's foe wasn't Kur, but the demon Asag, the spawn of An and Ki, and who produced monstrous offspring with Kur. In yet other versions, Ninurta is replaced by Adad/Ishkur. Were they all dragons? Further research is required.

And speaking of Absu, we also find him in Babylonian myth. Tiamat was the primordial goddess of the sea, mating with Absu, the god of fresh water, giving birth to new gods. Called the "glistening one," Tiamat was also known as the prime creator of chaos, and she is described as turning into a sea serpent or a dragon to wreak vengeance when her husband is killed. She is killed but before dying she brings forth the first monsters of the ancient Mesopotamian myths, including the first dragons with poison in their veins instead of blood. This would include Kur and/or Asag. A mother's revenge includes transformation.

The sea-serpent we also know as the ouroboros (and also as a variation of the dragons we're looking at in this work) is a symbol depicting a serpent or dragon eating its own tail, most likely first seen in ancient Egypt. The bitey serpent entered western tradition via Greek tradition and later through the tradition of alchemy. The symbol eventually became to symbolize introspection. The ouroboros also represents never-ending creation and destruction.

The first known appearance of the ouroboros is in an Egyptian funerary text (yes, as in the Egyptian Book of the Dead). Two serpents are shown holding their tails in their mouths, winding themselves around the mighty Ra. The serpents protect the god in his underworld journey, representing the beginning and the end of time.

The ouroboros also appears elsewhere in Egyptian texts, representing disorder amid order. The symbol is involved in periodic renewal and persisted into the Roman period, appearing on emblems denoting magical matters.

The original title of this workshop was "Here, There Be Dragons." This is a phrase we've all read, and it comes from the cartographers of an earlier time. That's what they wrote at the end of the known world. But where did the mapmakers get the phrase?

Probably from the ancient Greeks. According to them, the ancients believed the unknown parts of the world were inhabited by creatures they referred to as *dracones*. (Let's ignore the fact that the dragons they theorized as being in those parts would have been a surprise to the locals.) They opined that the types were:

Ethiopian: Giant serpents in Africa (specifically sub-Saharan Africa).

Indian: Dragons in the hills and mountains of India. They were thought to gobble elephants and to do battle with local dragon-slayers with the aid of some magic. (More on the dragons of India in the next chapter.)

Phrygian: Sixty-foot tall dragons in central Anatolia, now known as Asia Minor (the Asian part of Turkey). These dragons stood on their tails, catching birds for snacks with their magical breath. (Fiery? Poisonous? Further research is required.)

The Greeks had determined there were four types of dragons:

Dracones (from which our word "dragon" was derived)
Serpentine, lots of scary teeth, magical powers (some had 'em, some didn't), poison (most), and usually had multiple heads from a couple to hundreds.

There are many dracones in myth and legend. The Colchian dracon guarded the famous golden fleece and gave the hero Jason a pretty hard time, although he finally triumphed. Demeter, the goddess of the harvest, had a chariot drawn by dracones. Since they're described as snakelike, how they did this with no legs is a mystery. Not only that, Heracles slew the Hesperian dracon. You can find dracones mentioned all over Greek mythology and legend.

Cetus
This term is now the scientific name for whales. Yes, dragons were sea-monsters. Didn't we mention that?

Poseidon, not at all happy with the Aepiopians, sent a cetus to take care of things. Loyal to Poseidon and a bit on the hungry side, the cetus wasn't about to let go of a free princess meal. But alas for the cetus and hoorah for Princess Andromeda, Perseus did away with the monster. We wonder if he got the girl. Not the only time a cetus battled a Greek hero, because elsewhere, Heracles (again) overcame the Trojan cetus.

Chimera

These version of dragons had the front body of a lion, rear quarters of a goat, goat's head protruding from the back, goat's udder on the belly, and a serpent's tail. They also breathed fire.

The chimera used the people and sheep of Lykia as its food source, and they didn't much like it (the people *or* the sheep). The hero Bellerophon, mounted on the winged horse Pegasus, killed the vicious beast by driving a spear down its throat—a tricky deed when the beast in question can barbecue you. But he did, and he triumphed.

Remember St. George's dragon? The most famous painting depicting the dragon was actually a chimera.

Other chimerae: Nemeian lion, the Sphinx (yes, we know it's Egyptian, but still). And finally:

Dracaenae

These were female dragons, and these females were definitely not to be messed with! They had the top body and head of a beautiful nymph, but instead of legs, they had a serpent's tail, similar to the dracones. And they were fierce indeed, according to the stories.

The Greeks had lots of dracaena, and one reason was the fertile Echidna. According to the oldest descriptions, Echnidna, associated with Hesiod and the daughter of sea-gods, was a she-dragon with the head and bust of a woman, and represented the horrors of the earth—rot, fetid slime, unclean waters, sea-scum, illness, disease. Also referred to as the Tartarean *lamprey* (not to be mistaken with the Bulgarian *lamya*, a hydra-like thing), they decided she was the denizen of Tartarus, dark and deep beneath. Together with her consort, a storm-demon named Typhoeus, they gave birth to terrible monsters.

All roads lead to Rome
And all dragons, too. If the Romans didn't have something in their own mythologies, they took it from someone else. In the case of dragons, they borrowed myths and legends from Greece and Egypt. The stories are pretty much the same, but the Romans used different names, just as they renamed most of the Greek gods, goddesses, and heroes they appropriated.

We readily admit that we gave Roman dragons short shrift in our research because we kept running into versions of the same Greek stories over and over.

Dragons appeared in Greek and Roman myths both. Apollo fought the dragon Python, which guarded the Delphi oracle. In both sets of myth and legend, dragons were thought to know the secrets of the earth (knowledge being as valuable as gold and jewels, at least back then). Dragons of Greek and Roman myths had protective and fearsome qualities, and as a result, they were used as a military symbol. Roman soldiers of the first century crafted dragons on the standards that they carried into battle.

As we travel east, there's the Persian version of the dragon, mentioned in Zoroastrian scripture, in which stories include both positive *and* negative stories about dragons—remember, Persia is a gateway culture, with influences from both East and West. But there's a curious inversion, commented on by comparative linguistic and folklore academics: Many things viewed as negative in Persian mythology is topsy-turvy positive in Hindu mythology, with names that are clearly connected, so their roots in Indo-European myths are pretty apparent.

Over the millennia, the Persian, Afghani, and Indian cultures were involved in trading, territorial disputes, and war depending on who was in power, so the cultures, languages, and myths have a lot in common. More on that in the next chapter.

Consider this: If you had to, what dragon lore would you create, using all the various European dragon myths you had at your disposal?

Chinese dragon

Chapter 4
Dragons of India and China

And let's hop from Persia to India. Now we're talking about water dragons!

As opposed to the dragon legends of the West, the dragons of the East are usually water-based, associated with rainfall and bodies of water as well as fertility, usually wingless, serpentine, often positive, often seen as an authority figure, and still very much part of contemporary culture. But the Vedic version in Hindu myth goes along with the negative view of dragons we've seen in Persian myths in the form of the three-headed enemy of the Vedic hero.

Varuna, the Vedic god of storms, is regarded as the king of the *naga*, the local version of the dragon. The naga is the personification of drought and the enemy of Indra, the hero of Hindu sagas. Naga, also known as a snake-spirit, guarded the underground city of Bhagovati and its great treasures, just like so many stories in Western myths about dragons. They also hold the secret of immortality, so they guard treasures of all kinds.

These forms of dragons can take human form and many ancient tribes claimed to be descendants of the naga, especially from a union between a human hero and a feminine form of the snake called the *nagini*. Today, there are tribes that call themselves Nagas. The Japanese word for "long" is *nagai*. Coincidence? You decide.

The naga is often regarded as a deity in many Hindu cultures, and the king cobra is one of the images you'll find when you look for naga. (The term is a loose one, though, since human tribes are known as nagas, elephants are referred to as nagas, and just snakes in general.)

In the Mahabharata, a major Hindu epic, nagas are the enemy, referred to as "persecutors of all creatures," poisonous, strong, and intent on biting others. They're also important in many of the stories, but no more evil nor deceitful than other characters, and even good from time to time, with a cross between human and serpent characteristics. One example is the naga prince Sesha, who was entrusted by Brahma himself to balance the world on his head. To humans they're malevolent only if they are mistreated by humans, and that includes damage to the environment, making them protectors of nature as well.

In many Buddhist countries, the naga myth merges with local stories of the great serpents. You don't hear about snakes being great and wise in the West, mainly because snakes are the Enemy, thanks to Biblical tradition. So if you run across snake stories in East Asian legends, they won't have anything to do with that apple and snake story you remember from Bible class!

The Buddhist version of the naga generally also takes the form of a great cobra, usually with a single head but sometimes with many. In Buddhist paintings, the naga is sometimes shown as a human being with a snake or dragon extending from his head, but not his head in itself. Naga are believed to live among the other deities as well as in various parts of the human-inhabited earth, water, and underground caverns. There's also a naga who is the protector of the Buddha.

Then there are those Chinese dragons. Oh, those Chinese dragons!

In China, the naga was viewed as being equal with the Chinese dragon, though not the same. If you know anything about Chinese culture, you know that dragons are integral to the society. The Chinese dragon was the symbol of Chinese emperors (with a commonly cited life span of about 3,500 years)(the phoenix was the symbol of the empress, just in case you're curious, thus the reference to the dragon and phoenix thrones). Chinese dragons are most similar to those found in the rest of East Asia, specifically Japanese, Korean, Vietnamese, and Bhutanese ones, but with local variations. (As an example, in Bhutanese dragon myths, the thunder dragon is known as "druk" and is regarded as a national symbol.)

Chinese dragons are also serpentine, but with four legs, so a snake with four legs. In Chinese mythology, if you're familiar with the concept of yin and yang, a dragon represents yang and the phoenix represents yin. Dragons are good guys here, powerful and strong, filled with good luck, a symbol of imperial power. To say that someone is a dragon is a very good thing, even though there are occasional references to the same streak of orneriness that we see in Indian naga culture.

The Chinese dragon has specific categories. In various dynasties throughout the millennia, the golden and five-clawed dragon was the symbol of the emperor, also referred to as the Son of Heaven; the four-clawed dragon was the symbol of the nobility; and the three-clawed ones to the bureaucrats. The four- and three-claws were sometimes also assigned to the commoners, but those five-claws were always for the royals. In any case, the term "descendants of the dragon" has been used by the Chinese in general to refer to themselves.

So how long have dragons been a big deal in China? At least 7,000 years, if the discovery of a dragon statue from around the fifth millennium BCE is any clue. Dinosaur bones discovered were assumed to be those of dragons, of course, the way they were in other places. More on that later.

In Chinese mythology, the dragon has very much expanded abilities. It can disguise itself, it can fly, it can form into clouds, it can turn into water, and in some subcultures, dragons are said to have all the attributes of the other members of the twelve-symbol Chinese zodiac.

There are four dragon kings according to Chinese legend, each representing one of the known seas in traditional Chinese culture—again, the connection with water, including weather. In fact, the king of Wu-Yue in the Five Dynasties and Ten Kingdoms period was referred to as the "Sea Dragon King" because of his work in bringing water to his people. And as a good example of how myths can echo from culture to culture, in some Chinese legends, an emperor born with a birthmark in the shape of a dragon foretells the overthrow of the existing dynasty and the founding of a new one, while another legend tells of a prince in hiding who is identified by, again, his dragon birthmark. So do you know someone who does? Hm.

Next chapter, we'll take a look how the dragon myth has spread and changed throughout the rest of Asia.

Consider this: Are you ever going to look at a snake the same way again?

The Vietnamese dragon is most often a combination of crocodile, snake, cat, rat…and maybe more!

Chapter 5
Dragons of the "More"

It's safe to say that the dragons of the rest of Asia have a large part of their origins from India and China. But as we wander a bit from the Silk Road and start to explore the rest of Asia (we've come this far, why not?), we can see how those myths of India and China began to evolve for those areas.

In the warmer areas of Asia, the myths of dragons as *naga* are most prominent. In Malaysia, naga are commonly shown as a dragon with many heads, while in Laos the legends say the naga are often shown as water serpents with beaks. In Thailand, the water dragon, which is mainly known as the *phaya naga*, is regarded as a holy creature and worshipped.

Now, the phaya naga is your basic king of the mythical creatures in these parts, with amazing powers as described in local folklore. There is a particular forest in Thailand that is said to be the border between our world and the netherworld, and is where the phaya naga reigns. (It's also said to be haunted.) The belief in the phaya naga is sometimes likened to those in the Loch Ness monster in Scotland or the ogopogo in Canada, except the belief in these parts is stronger.

Cambodian myths also have the naga in their culture, with stories about an ancient empire hidden in a lake and a kingdom in the nearby part of the ocean. One of the Cambodian origin stories, in fact, says that the daughter of the naga king married a human man, and that's how the Cambodian people came into existence, and why they refer to themselves as having been born of the naga.

The Mekong River and the legend of the naga are very strongly connected and part and parcel of the Thai and Laotian legends. The naga are still believed to rule the river, and annual sacrifices are still held for them, because locals believe that the naga can protect them from danger. Not only that, there is a yearly sighting in a Thai province, on the night of the fifteenth day of the eleventh month in the Laotian lunar calendar, in which fireballs seem to rise from the Mekong. Villagers believe that the naga in the Mekong shoot the fireballs into the air to celebrate the end of a period sometimes referred to as the "Buddhist Lent," which is a three-month retreat that takes place during the rainy season (usually July to October).

During this period, believers give up meat, alcohol, and smoking during this time and they meditate. The naga sightings seen during this period, of a 60-foot serpent with black-green scales, could be based on a local giant snake indigenous to the area.

Some well-known naga include the Ananta-Sesha, the world snake with a thousand heads; Karkotaka, who controls the weather; Mucalinda, who protects the Buddha; Padmavati, the naga queen; and Paravataksha, whose sword causes earthquakes.

While the Cambodian origin myth has the people

descending from a naga princess and a human man, the Vietnamese creation myth has the people the product of a dragon and a faery.

According to the story, the king of the dragons married a goddess, the daughter of the bird king. The daughter produced 100 eggs, which hatched into 100 sons and established the Vietnamese people, thus giving birth to the old Vietnamese proverb, "Children of the dragon, grandchildren of the gods." (We can hear you now: Yes, but what about the women? More research is required.)

In Vietnamese myth, the dragon is often the combined image of crocodile, snake, cat, rat, and bird. The dragon is perhaps the most important, symbolizing such power that it can spit a vapor so deadly that it can turn into water *or* fire. Here, the dragon is the symbol of man, the phoenix the woman. (These two, along with the tortoise and the unicorn, are the four most important symbols of the Vietnamese culture. And of course, the dragon is the symbol of the emperor in China, with the phoenix the symbol of the empress.) Marriage is represented when the two creatures are together in art or designs.

Further, the dragon creates or is involved in the creation of meteors, and is often considered to the god of the waters. It's safe to say that this is a good representation of the many different kinds of influences coming into play in this region, sort of the Asian version of the gateway culture we've seen in Persia.

In a sharp difference from the serpentine image of the dragon that we've seen previously, the Vietnamese dragon is an ever-changing combination of crocodile, snake, lizard, and bird, but for the most part a water deity. The dragon also has been described as having the horns of a deer, the head of a camel, and the scales of a fish. Also the hide of a water buffalo. So pretty much anything you can imagine!

As you may have gathered, there are huge variations in dragon types in Asia, depending on region and dynasty. In some times and areas, the dragon seen in art and imagery is short, with a cat-like body and a fish's back fin, while in other dynasties and places, a dragon more in line with the Chinese version is more common, with slender, flowing bodies, very serpentine, with fins (but rarely any limbs). Arms and horns came to define the Vietnamese dragon around the early 1400s, but with three claws. Five claws came later, with the heads of lions.

Beware the power of the dragon in this region! That reminder is never far from the minds of the people, as can be ascertained with the explanation behind the red tinge of certain rivers. A sleeping dragon was wounded when a military general tried to eliminate the blockage of a river with use of poorly arranged explosives. The dragon's wound never healed, and in the dragon's fury, the region suffered from drought and floods alternatively for years afterward. So as the old saying goes, let sleeping dragons lie!

And in Vietnamese myth as in China, certain fish cannot be eaten. The story goes that certain rites can transform a three-year-old carp into a dragon. As a result, the Vietnamese avoid eating large carp, particularly if they are black or dark, to avoid disaster.

Then there are Korean dragons, the style of which is heavily influenced by the Chinese version but also unique to their culture and environment—for instance, Korean legends refer to talking dragons. The Korean dragon very specifically has a beard, like the Chinese dragon, but a longer one. On occasion the dragon may be shown carrying a gem in its claws, which can also be seen in other Asian dragons—the Chinese, the Vietnamese, even the Bhutanese.

But the Korean myth holds that the dragon who held the gem would have certain unique powers of creation, but only four-toed dragons (with thumbs to hold onto the gem) could hold on to the jewel (the three-toed dragon wouldn't be able to, not having an opposable thumb).

Korean dragon myths hold that there are levels of dragons, with lesser dragons resembling enormous serpents. One of these dragons could become a true, higher-level dragon if it caught one of the gems that had fallen from heaven.

Next, we'll look at Japanese dragons!

Consider this: Do you think that the croc-headed dragon with wings would be an interesting character? Fun to draw?

Japanese dragon

Chapter 6
Land of the Rising Dragon

As you might expect by now, Japanese dragons have a lot in common with the dragons of the rest of Asia, but as you might also expect by now, they do have their differences. The dragons of Japan are a lot like the Chinese dragons in appearance, but not identical. Yes, they are both water gods, connected with rainfall and lakes and rivers and fertility, usually seen as very big, wingless, serpents with clawed feet (three, four, or five, depending on the story being told and where). The Chinese dragons are more serpentine, however, while the Japanese dragons have spines on their backs. And in Japanese dragon mythology, like other regions, there are both positive and negative points, even a reference to the Dragon's Triangle, the Asian equivalent of the Bermuda Triangle, less than 100 miles south of Tokyo.

The first references to dragons in Japanese culture can be found in the oldest of Japanese texts. In the ancient, classical work Kojiki, there's an eight-headed and eight-tailed dragon fought and bested by Susanoo, the god of wind and sea, and there are also stories about dragon shapeshifters, turning into humans as well as other creatures. Then there's Ryujin, the sea god or dragon god, who lives in a palace under the sea, where he keeps gems that can control the tides.

As in some of the other Asian dragon lore we're looked at, Japanese dragons are also considered to be the founders of the society itself. Toyotama-hime, the princess daughter of Ryujin, is considered to be the ancestor of Emperor Jimmu, the founding emperor of Japan (approximately 600 BCE), so yes, they regard themselves as yet again "children of the dragon." And again like other dragon myths around Asia, these dragons are benevolent unless you annoy them, so references to sacrifices to the local dragon deity are common. (We've read maidens for sacrifices, we've read rice and wine too, so those are common all over the world. We've even read stories in which those to be sacrificed are willing so all of life could be spared.)

Again like the other dragons found in Asia, there are other indications that the indigenous marine life may have played into the formation of the dragon myth. The *wani* was a sea monster, according to Japanese historical texts, which translates as modern-day descriptions of shark and crocodile, so while there aren't any crocs in Japan, clearly the locals must have known about them from more southern countries.

Many Japanese dragon names or words referring to dragons are terms taken from Chinese, but not all. For instance, of two common words that mean "dragon" in Japanese, one, *ryu*, is of Chinese origin, while the other, *tatsu*, is a native Japanese term. The Japanese also have a legend about the dragon kings who rule the four seas, so they adapted that from the Chinese too. But like the parallel stories of the Chinese weaving maiden and the Japanese star princess, sometimes you actually have to read the stories themselves to confirm what folktale is connected with which culture.

Later on, Buddhist monks from mainland Asia brought over Buddhism as well as dragon and snake legends to Japan, so the naga tales (you may recall from our earlier chapter that the Japanese word for "long" is *nagai*, so you can draw your own conclusions about that) brought over from Hindu myths became very much a reinterpretation of the earlier dragon-serpent stories in this new place and time. In Japanese myth, the tale about the dragon god Ryujin's tide-controlling jewels are remarkably similar to the naga's "wish-fulfilling" jewels back in India. The tale of the naga king who guarded the Buddha has the naga represented as a giant cobra—not the most positive image for Westerners, but for those looking at Eastern lore, it can be quite positive.

(But then, the Hindu goddess Sarasvati killed a three-headed serpent in ancient Vedic texts, while in the Japanese version of the same goddess, Benzaiten/Benten created an island to fight a five-headed dragon that had been threatening local villagers. If you go to Enoshima Island, an amusement area off the old Japanese military capital of Kamakura, south of Tokyo, even today, you'll find a statue commemorating the event. The goddess is often shown as riding on a good dragon, going to the rescue of humans being picked on by those mean dragons. Again, both positive and negative.)

In Japan, dragon mythology is usually connected with Buddhist temples and Shinto shrines. Even today, you'll find stories about shapeshifting dragons changing into the goddess of mercy, Kannon (the Chinese version is Kwan-Yin). The names of temples are often dragon related. There's the Heavenly Dragon Temple, Dragon Swamp Temple, and Dragon Peace Temple, just to name three.

Legend has it that a famous Buddhist temple in Tokyo, Senso-ji, was founded when a golden statuette of Kannon was found in a nearby river, and the temple was built around the statuette to hide it away from humans, and somewhere in there golden dragons appeared and made their way up into the heavens. Beautiful temple; take a visit the next time you're in town. No dragons around, though.

But then, consider this. In Chinese dragon lore, the dragon represents the emperor and the phoenix represents the empress, while in Japanese dragon lore, the dragon and the phoenix are ancient, sworn enemies. So there are definitely differences!

Finally, water and dragons are very much found together in Japanese folklore, for good or ill. The Dragon's Triangle, also known as the Devil's Sea (also the Formosa Triangle), is an area about 60 miles or so south of Tokyo. This region seems to be very big or quite small, depending on where you read about it, and it's very much the local equivalent of the Bermuda Triangle. (This illustration is approximate, in case you hadn't guessed. It would make more sense if it were a little farther south than 60 miles, but that's the thing about myths: They're malleable.)

Approximate area of the Dragon's Triangle.

According to Charles Berlitz's books *The Bermuda Triangle* and *The Dragon's Triangle*, this region is dangerous for sailors. Berlitz states that Japan lost a number of military and government vessels there in the 1950s, losing more than 800 people before the area was officially declared a danger zone. And it's not just military; over the years, fishing boats, pleasure cruises, and more have been lost in the region. Speculation had it that it could have been underwater eruptions with the volcanoes still active in the Japanese archipelago, and there are legends that the dragons who have their lair below the water come up and smite those who disturb their sleep, so it's very logical to call it the "Dragon's Triangle." Or at least we think so.

Consider this: Would you go to an amusement park devoted to dragons?

Javanese dragon-bird

Chapter 7
Fierce Fighter Dragons of Asia Pacific

The Asia Pacific dragons are still the water-based creatures you see all over the Far East, but the farther east we go, the more and more you read about dragons that sound distinctly crocodile-like, giving more credence to the theory that the dragon myth comes from referring to an unfamiliar reptile as a dragon.

While stories about other Asian dragons refer to their powers of control over the various forms of water, the Philippine *bakunawa* is the first one we've run into that is said to actually cause eclipses. It's also said to have a mouth the size of a lake, a red tongue, whiskers and gills, and not one but two sets of wings. (Quick, what does a catfish look like? Go ahead and take a look. We'll wait.)

There are also other serpent or dragon deities you see references to in the region, which make sense because there are dozens of indigenous peoples in the area, complete with their own myths. The Tagalog stories are the ones we found most often, though.

The story behind this particular dragon and its ability to cause eclipses is made even more intriguing because in early Filipino tales, there were originally seven moons created by Bathala, the Creator of All Things, in the evening sky, and when the moons were full, the dragon, so transfixed by their beauty, would rise from the sea and swallow them. This ticked off Bathala, understandably. To prevent this from happening again and again, the locals would have to scare the bakunawa into spitting the moons back out, either making noises using pots and pans and drums or playing soothing instruments to make the dragon fall asleep and allow them to kill it. This was an iffy proposition, though, so the bakunawa was known as both a moon-eater and a man-eater. But we're now left with a single moon, so they must have succeeded.

There's also another story in which the bakunawa rose from the ocean and ate the moon to punish the people for killing his sister the sea turtle, and again they had to make a lot of noise to make the dragon throw up the moon. So what can we gather from these stories? First, the locals definitely connected the bakunawa dragons with the disappearance of the moon (as in eclipses, which definitely goes along with the ability of the dragons elsewhere in the Asian region to control the tides), and second, making a lot of noise would cause the dragon to regurgitate the moon. We can only conclude that the bakunawa didn't like a lot of noise or threw up easily. But the stories also say that the dragons disappeared afterward, so take that as you will.

Bakunawa may have vanished from the earthly realm we inhabit, but their influence remains. The hilts of ancient Filipino swords have images of dragon's heads, the image of which is supposed to bestow great power when the swords are used in combat.

Then there are the *taniwha* dragons of New Zealand, which were supposed to be for the most part dangerous and evil creatures who could disappear to parts unknown (assumed to be another plane of existence or world). The descriptions of the taniwha made them sound alternately like whales, fish, eels, and lizards, so we can't help but consider there might have been a translation glitch somewhere.

But there was apparently a particular kind of taniwha dragon called the *ngarara* that made the European explorers think of their own version of dragons. The ngarara didn't have wings or the fiery breath that western European versions usually are described as having, but it had big jaws with a whole lot of teeth, hard scaly skin with spines along the back (like the Japanese dragon), a long, dangerous tail, and it also was a man-eater. So by the time we get to this part of the world, the dragons are sounding remarkably familiar and much less fantastical. Crocodiles are rare, but not unheard of in that region; a particular type has been found as far as the Fiji islands.

We didn't find as many dragon references in Hawaiian folklore as we did in other Pacific Rim cultures, but we did find one offhand notation in which the local shark god, Kauhuhu, has his home on a high ocean cliff, protected by a couple of Hawaiian dragons. This appears to be another example of how sharks and dragons seem to be closely related in terrorizing and mystifying the humans who come too close to them.

And with that, we're pretty much finished with the Asian dragons. Now, what about possible dragon origins? Check out our next chapter!

Consider this: How do you think the descriptions of dragons changed the way they did around Asia?

Chapter 8
Dragon Theories and Origins

We've looked at a lot of dragons, all different kinds. If you've read the descriptions of the dragons from various cultures and countries, you'll have noticed, of course, that the way the dragons are described changes from region to region, culture to culture. You've no doubt noticed that the western dragons seem to have not much in common with the eastern dragons, until we get to the easternest eastern we could go east (heading east, that is), when the descriptions of dragons got to sound downright familiar (but not called dragons in the West). Does that mean there aren't really any dragons in those parts of the world, and they were instead called dragons instead of crocodiles or giant catfish or whatever? Nope, that's not it at all.

Well, it's like this. Every culture's dragon represents something unique to that culture. Sometimes those dragons are good, protectors of the people, and sometimes those dragons are wicked and evil, and must be killed (or converted to Christianity, as in the case of the alternate endings of the St. George story; there are also corresponding stories about an obstreperous dragon being converted to Buddhism in the East. So dragons are redeemable if you don't go and kill them). Sometimes those dragons can fly and have wings; sometimes they're sea serpents and are seen nowhere near the skies. Sometimes in the East they're more like snakes, but not in the West, because the snake represents evil incarnate there. Sometimes the dragons have five claws, or four, or three, or none at all, depending on where and when you are and if those claws are symbolic of social status. Sometimes the descriptions of dragons sound remarkably like giant catfish. Sometimes the descriptions of dragons sound remarkably like giant crocodiles. But in any case, there are stories about creatures referred to as dragons.

What all this told us was maybe, just maybe, there might have been a giant reptile of some kind at one time, where the stories first began, at the dawn of human history, in different areas of the world. It might have been more than one creature, maybe related, maybe not. And if there wasn't, perhaps the skeletons of such made their way back along the Silk Road as curiosities, giving rise to the fantastical stories. Definitely reptilian, that's for sure.

The Vietnamese dragon combines aspects of the crocodile, snake, lizard, and bird. Vietnamese culture thrived near rivers, so it makes sense the croc was highly venerated. The snake is highly regarded in not-so-far-away India, so the snake part makes sense too. And the bird? Still not out of the question. The modern-day bird and the long-ago dinosaur are supposed to be kin, after all, and dinosaur bones are supposed to be what's left of dragons, according to one theory. And those descriptions of Quetzalcoatl and its feathers? Guess what's one of the theories about some of those dinosaurs? Yep, you guessed it. Dragons and feathers!

Further, images of what could have been drawings of dragons have been found in the Southeast Asian region, often seen with a crocodile head but with the body of the snake. Then there's an image of something that looks like a cat and a dragon combined—the head's not that of a croc, it has more of a feline look to it, with a long neck. But that was identified as a dragon too. It's a handy all-around term.

And crocodiles are mentioned frequently in some tales involving dragons, wherever we go. The descriptions of these creatures in the more tropical climates of the Pacific Rim get wilder and more exotic the farther north and west we go, and it would make sense to consider the idea that their skeletons, brought back as yet another example of the wonders to be found along the Silk Road, inspired the myths. (Yes, we just mentioned this, but give it some thought.)

Certainly the references to dragons in the Pacific Rim sound like crocs (or like giant catfish). Just because we don't associate crocs with those particular descriptions doesn't mean they didn't exist at one point. That's one thing about the jungles of the Pacific Rim, and the depths of the Pacific Ocean; we know many things, but we don't know everything.

And speaking of which, there's the lionfish (*pterois*), found mostly in the Pacific Rim but can also be found these days in the Atlantic, which comes in many varieties but is probably best known for being aquarium favorites. They're colorful, with spiky fins and poisonous spines. That poison can cripple and incapacitate adult humans (and even kill kids, the elderly, and the sick).

The venomous spines of the lionfish may have been one of the reasons that stories about dragons and their deadly bite came about, at least in the East. Apparently some varieties are edible, with a taste not unlike grouper.

Can you imagine that, being able to say you ate dragon?

Finally, speaking of poison, there's the creature known as a dragon that actually exists today, also known as the monitor lizard. The Komodo dragon of Indonesia, growing as big as six and a half to almost ten feet, has a unique aspect to it that might have given some inspiration to the fire-breathing dragon stories: Its saliva has poisonous bacteria that can cause a crippling, fatal infection, so if it were to bite something, the feeling would feel like a burn—like fire. Apparently there's no antidote, so keep away. There are other creatures with a bite that can poison and burn, so the idea about the fiery breath certainly has merit.

There's nothing to say that there wasn't an earlier version of the Komodo, bigger, with slightly different features, maybe even wings, vestigial or not. Remember those reports about the fossil record of hobbit people of Indonesia? Stories about a tiny people in the Pacific were assumed to be myths of the region, until the fossil remains of a small, heretofore unknown people were found. Keep in mind that there's a small flying lizard that's been in the news in recent years, and we could swear that it looks just like a dragon of our myths and legends. Or that could be a hoax. But since it's in the Pacific Rim region, it's hard to say. Big area, lots of unknown still. And we must be challengers of the unknown.

Maybe the myth of the dragon goes back even farther. One reference we found speculated that perhaps comet impact was the origin of the dragon myths. Why not? Remember, one of the depictions of dragons was as serpents with wings and that they could fly through the sky, sort of like a comet. Dragons were often described as having a reptilian head and a long body, right? Comets must have been a wondrous thing to earlier mankind, with a flaming head and a long body, flying through the sky. The myths of the dragons could have certainly had their start there. Remember, just because we don't know about it now doesn't mean we didn't know about back then—nor will we know about it in the future.

Consider this: Which of the origin theories sound most likely to you?

Summary
And Draggin' In, Finally

We've looked at dragons around the world. We can agree that the world's an amazing place, filled with creatures we can both imagine and we can't—and that may yet exist, just somewhere beyond our knowledge. If nothing else, they exist in our imaginations, and that's the place to start. All the information we've given you here should be a starting point for you to fuel your stories and give them texture.

We tend to think dragons emerged as chimera creatures, all the most wondrous parts of things slapped together, kind of like a Michael Bay film ("More explosions! And robots! And flying exploding robots! And hot chicks that turn into flying exploding robots!")

On top of this, from a Jungian perspective, can dragons reflect our awareness of our deep fears, both of the world and our own shadow impulses? We fear the dragon within and externalize it. After all, water is tied to the un- and subconscious.

Tell us what you've taken away from our trip around the world. Does a particular account about a dragon resonate with you? Go forth and hunt for your own dragons!

Eilis and Jacquie

Bibliography

Appiah, Kwame Anthony, and Henry Louis Gates Jr. [1996]. *Dictionary of Global Culture*, Borzoi Books: Alfred A. Knopf, Inc.

Arrowsmith, Nancy, and George Morse [1977]. *A Field Guide to the Little People*, Macmillan.

Ashe, Geoffrey [1985]. *The Discovery of King Arthur*, Anchor Press/Doubleday.

Berlitz, Charles [1974]. *The Bermuda Triangle*, Wynwood Press.

_______ [1989]. *The Dragon's Triangle*, Wynwood Press.

Bradley, Åsa Maria [2015]. *Viking Warrior Rising*, Sourcebooks.

Briggs, Katharine [1977]. *British Folktales*, Pantheon Books.

Campbell, Joseph [1988]. *Myths to Live By*, Bantam Books.

Cavendish, Richard, ed. [1970]. *Man, Myth & Magic: An Illustrated Encyclopedia of the Supernatural*, Marshall Cavendish Corp.

Conway, D.J. [2001]. *Magickal, Mystical Creatures*, Llewellyn Publications.

Cotterell, Arthur [1996]. *Illustrated Encyclopedia of Classical Mythology*, Hermes House.

Curran, Bob [2009]. *Werewolves*, New Page Books.

Curtis, Vesta Sarkhosh [1933]. *Persian Myths*, University of Texas Press.

Davis, F. Hadland [1989]. *Myths & Legends of Japan*, Graham Brash Ltd.

Davisson, Zack [2017]. *Supernatural Cats of Japan*, Chin

Music Press.

Dieterle, Richard [2005]. *Short Encyclopedia of Hotcâk (Winnebago) Myth, Legend, and Folklore*, publisher unknown.

Flynn, Elizabeth MS [2017]. "Lafcadio Hearn: The Man Behind the Plaque," Noladefender.com, July 7.

Foster, Michael Dylan [2015]. *The Book of Yokai: Mysterious Creatures of Japanese Folklore*, University of California Press.

Fuller, Edmund [1974]. *Mythology by Thomas Bulfinch*, Dell Publishing.

Graves, Robert [1960]. *The Greek Myths*, Pelican.

Hamel, Frank [2007]. *Werewolves, Bird-Women, Tiger-Men and Other Human Animals*, Dover Publications.

Hamilton, Edith [1969]. *Mythology*, Warner Books.

Haughton, Brian [2008]. *Lore of the Ghost: The Origins of the Most Famous Stories Throughout the World*, New Page Books.

Hearn, Lafcadio [2007]. *Chita: A Memory of Last Island*, Echo Library.

_______ [2005]. *Kwaidan: Stories and Studies of Strange Things.* Boston: Tuttle.

_______ [2011]. *La Cuisine Creole: A Collection of Culinary Recipes*, Applewood Books.

Ions, Veronica [1992]. *Indian Mythology*, Reed International Books.

Iwasaka, Michiko, and Barre Toelken [1994]. *Ghosts and the Japanese: Cultural Experience in Japanese Death Legends*, Utah State University, University Libraries.

Katz, Brian P. [1995]. *Deities and Demons of the Far East*, MetroBooks.

Knight, Sirona [2005]. *Complete Idiot's Guide to Elves and Fairies*, Penguin Group.

Koizumi, Setsu [1918]. *Reminiscences of Lafcadio Hearn.* New York: Macmillan. Translated by Paul Kiyoshi Hisada and Frederick Johnson.

Matthews, John [1999]. *The Barefoot Book of Giants, Ghosts, and Goblins*, Barefoot Books.

McCoy, Edain [2006]. *A Witch's Guide to Faery Folk*, Llewellyn Publications.

Murray, Alexander S. [1988]. *Who's Who in Mythology: A Classic Guide to the Ancient World*, Bracken Books.

Mythical Beasts [1996]. Anness Publishing, Ltd.

Sister Nivedita and Ananda K. Coomararswamy [1994]. *Hindus and Buddhists: Myths and Legends*, Guernsey Press.

Ralston, W.R.S. [1873]. *Russian Folk-Tales*, Elder and Co.

Schama, Simon [2000]. *A History of Britain: At the Edge of the World? 3000 BC to AD 1603*, Hyperion.

Storm, Rachel [2002]. *Asian Mythology*, Selectabook Ltd.

Wikipedia. Various entries.

Wilkinson, Philip [1998]. *Illustrated Dictionary of Mythology*, DK Publishing.

Yoda, Hiroko, and Matt Alt, translators [2016]. *Japandemonium Illustrated: The Yokai Encyclopedias of Toriyama Sekien*, Dover Publications.

Illustrations

Page 2: Silk Road map. Shutterstock

Page 8: Quetzalcoatl. Creative Commons license. Creator Eddo

Page 16: Courtesy of Creative Commons

Page 26: Courtesy of Creative Commons

Page 34: Chinese dragon. Dover Publications

Page 40: Vietnamese dragon. Dover Publications

Page 46: Japanese dragon. Dover Publications

Page 50: Dragon's Triangle, drawn by author

Page 52: Javanese dragon-bird. Dover Publications

Page 56: Dover Publications

Page 62: Clipart

Author Biographies

JACQUIE ROGERS is a multiple award–winning author of Western novels, but her first burning desire was to be a baseball announcer. While she hasn't made that career change happen yet, she *has* been a programmer, a cow milker, a political strategist, a rodeo queen, and a bookstore manager, but currently, she writes stories about another place, another time. Check them out at JacquieRogers.com!

ELIZABETH MS FLYNN, who writes as Eilis Flynn, has written fiction in the form of comic book stories, fantasies (romance, urban, and historical), and short stories. She's also a professional editor and has been for more than forty years, working with academia, technology, finance, genre fiction, and comic books. She can be reached at emsflynn.com (if you're looking for an editor) or at eilisflynn.com (if you're looking for a good read).

Connect with us online

Facebook: www.facebook.com/jacquie.rogers.author

Facebook: www.facebook.com/EilisFlynnAuthor

Jacquie Rogers's website: www.jacquierogers.com

Eilis Flynn's website: www.eilisflynn.com

Have any dragon stories you want to tell us about? Have any questions? Drop by at mythsalongthesilkroad.blogspot.com!